Going to Work ANIMAL EDITION · Going to Work ANIMAL EDITION · Going to Work ANIMAL EDITION · Going to Work ANIMAL EDITION

Going To Work
ANIMAL EDITION

Search-and-Rescue Animals

ABDO
Publishing Company

A Buddy **Book by**
Julie Murray

VISIT US AT
www.abdopublishing.com

Published by ABDO Publishing Company, 8000 West 78th Street, Edina, Minnesota 55439.

Copyright © 2009 by Abdo Consulting Group, Inc. International copyrights reserved in all countries. No part of this book may be reproduced in any form without written permission from the publisher. Buddy Books™ is a trademark and logo of ABDO Publishing Company.

Printed in the United States.

Coordinating Series Editor: Rochelle Baltzer
Editor: Sarah Tieck
Contributing Editor: Marcia Zappa
Graphic Design: Maria Hosley
Cover Photograph: *Fotosearch:* Thinkstock
Interior Photographs/Illustrations: *AP Photo:* Frederic J. Brown/AFP (p. 29), Hadar Cohen/Israeli Defense Force (p. 13), Alan Diaz, file (p. 7), Andreas Fischer (p. 19), M. Spencer Green (p. 24), Jack Sauer (p. 21), Rui Vieira/PA Wire URN:5605615/Press Association via AP Images (p. 25); *Getty Images:* Timothy Clary/AFP (p. 11), Joe Raedle (pp. 7, 27), Michael Rieger/FEMA (p. 23); *iStockPhoto:* Douglas Adams (p. 15), Terry J. Alcorn (p. 5), Günay Mutlu (p. 15) Jim Parkin (p. 17), Mark Rose (pp. 19, 30); *Photos.com:* Jupiter Images (pp. 9, 15).

Library of Congress Cataloging-in-Publication Data

Murray, Julie, 1969-
   Search-and-rescue animals / Julie Murray.
      p. cm. -- (Going to work. Animal edition)
   ISBN 978-1-60453-563-1
   1. Search dogs--Juvenile literature. 2. Rescue dogs--Juvenile literature. I. Title.

SF428.73M87 2009
636.7'0886--dc22

2008044273

Contents

Animals At Work

Going to work is an important part of life. At work, people use their skills to accomplish tasks and earn money.

Animals can have jobs, too. Many times, they complete tasks that human workers can't.

Some animals do search-and-rescue work. Their job is to find people who are missing. This is worthwhile work.

Dogs have many natural skills that make them good at searching for people. They save lives!

Helping Out

Search-and-rescue animals are specially trained workers. Dogs and horses are the most common of these animals.

Search-and-rescue animals accompany **emergency** workers. They look for people who are lost, trapped, or missing.

Search-and-rescue animals work in many different settings. Sometimes, dogs must climb through uneven piles of rubble (*above*). Other times, horses may have to make their way around damaged buildings and trees (*below*).

HISTORY LESSON

Some of the first search-and-rescue animals were Saint Bernard dogs. Around 1000 AD, a group of European **monks** trained them. The dogs rescued people lost in the steep, snowy Alps.

The Saint Bernards became famous for their rescues around 1750. Since then, more people have used these dogs for rescues.

Saint Bernards have also been called hospice dogs, holy dogs, and mountain dogs.

Did You Know?

Saint Bernards are large dogs. They can reach 200 pounds (91 kg)! They are known to be strong, kind, and friendly.

Did You Know?

Wilma Melville founded the National Disaster Search Dog Foundation. Melville and her dog searched for people after the Oklahoma City bombing. That's when she realized the need for search-and-rescue dog teams. This led her to start the foundation.

Over the years, people realized the value of search-and-rescue dogs. **Foundations** were created to support the use of these dogs.

The National **Disaster** Search Dog Foundation started shortly after the Oklahoma City **bombing** in 1995. This group trains dogs to work as rescuers. Today, it provides many dog teams for help during disasters.

On April 19, 1995, a bomb destroyed a federal building in Oklahoma. Many people were hurt or killed. Dogs helped search for people at the site.

Working Together

Some search-and-rescue animals are pets. Others are working animals. Search-and-rescue animals are trained to work in cities, neighborhoods, and wilderness areas.

Most dogs work with a trainer at least twice a week for a year. They become fast and strong. They practice manners, too.

Search-and-rescue dogs work as part of a team. Each dog has a human partner, or handler.

Life Savers

Dogs do many different types of search-and-rescue jobs. They are well suited for this work.

Dogs have strong noses, and they can separate scents. They also hear well and can see well in the dark. And, dogs can often move quicker than humans, even in unsafe or bad conditions.

Rottweilers (*top left*), golden retrievers (*top right*), Labrador retrievers (*bottom right*), and German shepherds (*bottom left*) are used as search-and-rescue dogs.

Every human has a scent. Other humans may not be able to smell it, but dogs can. Trainers teach search-and-rescue dogs to **focus** on a scent and find it.

Two search methods are trailing and air scenting. When trailing, a dog follows an exact scent on or near the ground. When air scenting, a dog sniffs the air to find a scent. Some dogs use one method. Others can use both.

To properly use the trailing method, a dog needs a piece of clothing or another scented object. This helps it know which scent to follow.

Into The Wild

Some search-and-rescue dogs find people in the wilderness. They can be called to fields, forests, deserts, or mountains. There, they may travel over land or water. The weather may be hot, cold, or rainy.

An avalanche happens when a large amount of snow falls down a mountainside. Avalanche dogs dig in the snow to find people who are trapped underneath. The dogs usually live and work near ski areas.

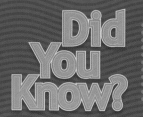
Search-and-rescue dogs aid humans. They save time during rescues.

In the wilderness, a dog can lead searchers to the area where a scent is strongest. This gives human workers a smaller space to search.

Some dogs can even find a person's scent in water!

RESCUE

Disaster Dogs

Some search-and-rescue dogs help out after fires or other **disasters**. They find people in noisy, dusty, and dark places.

When a building is **damaged**, people may be trapped inside. Disaster dogs are trained to find them quickly so doctors can help them.

On September 11, 2001, planes crashed into the World Trade Center in New York City, New York. Many people were killed or hurt. Search-and-rescue dogs looked for people trapped in the caved-in buildings.

In August 2005, Hurricane Katrina destroyed parts of the southern United States. Search-and-rescue dogs helped save people.

Search-and-rescue dogs also help after storms and natural **disasters**. They move through areas **damaged** by floods, **tornadoes**, and **earthquakes**. They help find people in need of rescue and doctors.

Sometimes, dogs wear special shoes during rescues. These shoes protect their paws from broken glass, rocks, or hot surfaces.

Hoofed Helpers

Horses are also used for search-and-rescue jobs. They can travel to areas where cars can't. They often search for people in the wilderness. And, they work in cities that have been destroyed by a **disaster**.

A horse and rider can travel far quickly. Horses are naturally aware of their surroundings. And, they are trained to **focus** on their work. They **alert** their riders to danger.

The size and strength of horses helps searchers. On horseback, searchers can see over bushes and small trees. And, they can carry rescued people to safety.

Gifted Workers

Search-and-rescue animals are important workers. They use their natural skills to save lives. These animals save more lives than human workers could save alone. Their special work makes the world a better place!

Search-and-rescue animals can move fast through unsafe places. They use their powerful senses to find people.

The Animal Times

Proving Their Worth

Before doing search-and-rescue work, animals and their handlers must be certified. This means they must prove they have passed the training.

Crime Fighters

Some search-and-rescue dogs work to solve crimes. Often, these dogs help find dead people. Dead bodies have a different scent than live bodies. So, the dogs search for that smell when working.

Important Words

alert (uh-LUHRT) to make someone aware of something.

bombing (BAHM-ihng) the action of being attacked with bombs. A bomb is a case filled with something that explodes when set off.

damage (DA-mihj) loss caused from harm done to a person or a property.

disaster (dih-ZAS-tuhr) an event that causes damage and suffering.

earthquake (UHRTH-kwayk) a shaking of a part of the earth.

emergency (ih-MUHR-juhnt-see) an unexpected event that requires immediate action.

focus (FOH-kuhs) to give attention to.

foundation (faun-DAY-shuhn) an organization that controls gifts of money and services.

monk (MUHNGK) a man who is part of a religious order whose members work and live together.

tornado (tawr-NAY-doh) a strong wind with a funnel-shaped cloud. A tornado moves in a narrow path over land.

Web Sites

To learn more about search-and-rescue animals, visit ABDO Publishing Company online. Web sites about search-and-rescue animals are featured on our Book Links page. These links are routinely monitored and updated to provide the most current information available.

www.abdopublishing.com

Index